AFFILIATE DISCLAIMER. The short, direct, non-legal version is this: Some of the links in this report may be affiliate links which means that I earn money if you choose to buy from that vendor at some point in the near future. I do not choose which products and services to promote based upon which pay me the most, I choose based upon my decision of which I would recommend to a dear friend. You will never pay more for an item by clicking through my affiliate link, and, in fact, may pay less since I negotiate special offers for my readers that are not available elsewhere.

DISCLAIMER AND/OR LEGAL NOTICES: The information presented herein represents the view of the author as of the date of publication. Because of the rate with which conditions change, the author reserves the right to alter and update his opinion based on the new conditions. The report is for informational purposes only. While every attempt has been made to verify the information provided in this report, neither the author nor his affiliates/partners assume any responsibility for errors, inaccuracies or omissions. Any slights of people or organizations are unintentional. If advice concerning legal or related matters is needed, the services of a fully qualified professional should be sought. This report is not intended for use as a source of legal or accounting advice. You should be aware of any laws which govern business transactions or other business practices in your country and state. Any reference to any person or business whether living or dead is purely coincidental.

Table of Contents

A Great Sales Page Makes It Rain

A great sales page is an absolutely essential part of any sales funnel. After all, a sales page is where you actually make a sale. It's where you convince someone to purchase your products or services. The sales page is what ultimately leads a person to open up their wallet, take out their credit card, and buy from you.

If you have a mediocre sales page, you simply won't make many sales. Nobody will want to purchase from you. Your conversion rate will be extremely low and your overall sales funnel will be highly ineffective.

A great sales page, on the other hand, causes your sales to skyrocket, dramatically increases your conversion rate, and turns leads into paying customers.

Simply put, your sales page can make or break you. Your revenue increases or falls based on the quality of your sales page.

Of course, all this raises a critical question: how do you create a great sales page?

If you're new to writing sales pages, it can seem kind of overwhelming. How do you communicate everything you need to in order to make the sale? How do you convince people to purchase from you? How do you overcome reluctance and demonstrate just how awesome your product or service really is?

Good news:

You can learn to create a great sales page.

In some ways, a sales page is formulaic. Every good sales page contains the same core elements. Sort of like a math equation. Once you learn what these core elements are and how they work, you can put them together to create a highly effective sales page.

In this book, you'll discover the secrets of creating a great sales page. We're going to reveal time-tested formulas and strategies that are guaranteed to increase sales and conversions.

As we go through each element of the sales page, you'll see how they work together. How they fit together like pieces of a puzzle. How each element builds upon and adds to the previous elements.

By the end, you'll be in a prime position to create your own killer sales page that converts like crazy.

Ready?

Let's get started.

Step #1: Understand Your Audience

Before you begin writing any elements of your sales page, it's absolutely critical that you understand your audience. The simple truth is that if you don't know who you're talking to, you won't be able to persuade them very effectively. You need to be able to talk directly to your audience in language that resonates with them.
One key to a great sales page is thoroughly knowing your audience.

Until you've taken the time to do a deep dive into your audience to understand what makes them tick, you can't get to work on your sales page. You need to be able to put yourself in your ideal customer's shoes. To be able to see things from their point of view. To know what they really want.

Once you know your audience, you can craft your sales page so that it connects on a deep, personal level with them.

What do you need to know about your audience?

Here are some simple questions to help you define your audience:

- What age are your primary customers?
- Are they primarily male, female, or a mix?
- What are their biggest pain points and challenges?
- What motivates them?
- What do they aspire to?
- What are their goals, hopes, and dreams?
- What do they fear?
- What have they tried in the past that hasn't worked?
- What objections do they have to purchasing from you?
- What makes them happy?
- Who are their biggest influences?
- What websites do they frequent?
- Who do they follow on social media?

Take the time to work carefully through all these questions. The end result will be a *buyer persona*. A buyer persona is a representation of your ideal customer. It's who you're trying to sell to. Ideally, your sales page should be written so that it speaks in ways that are familiar to your buyer persona.

It's okay if you end up with multiple customer personas. Your product or service might appeal to several different types of people.

The key is that you know exactly who you're selling to. Whether you have one persona or several, it's absolutely essential that you understand who will be reading your sales page and what makes them want to buy.

Step #2: Craft Your Headline

It's hard to overstate the importance of a sales page headline. The headline is what catches people's attention and draws them into the rest of your sales page. It's what convinces people to keep reading.

A boring headline will result in people quickly leaving your sales page, uninterested by what you have to offer. A good headline will immediately intrigue your readers, catch their interest, and make them want to read more.

Famous advertising copywriter, David Ogilvy, said:

> *On the average, five times as many people read the headline as read the body copy. When you have written your headline, you have spent eighty cents out of your dollar.*

In other words, your headline is critically important. It can make or break your sales page. Given the importance of your headline, you should take as long as necessary to craft a compelling, interesting, intriguing headline.

In order to create a compelling headline, you must know your Unique Selling Proposition (USP).

Your USP is what you *uniquely* have to offer your customers. It's your secret sauce. The thing that you're best at. It's how you help your customers succeed. Your USP sets you apart from your competitors and helps potential customers immediately understand what you have to offer them.

Here's a simple formula for determining your USP:

I help [PERSON] to [SPECIFIC RESULTS] by [YOUR SOLUTION]

For example, let's say you're a success coach who focuses on helping business owners grow their businesses through online marketing. Your USP could be, *I help small business owners double their leads by using digital marketing.*

Or maybe you're a fitness coach. Your USP could be something like, *I help middle-aged women achieve their weight loss goals with a unique combination of exercise and mindset shifts.*

Your sales page headline will flow out of your USP and be tailored specifically to the product or service you're selling.

Your headline should:

- Identify the specific problem your product or service solves
- State the big benefit
- Trigger emotion in the reader
- Intrigue the reader
- Convince the reader to check out the rest of the sales page

Here are some specific formulas you can use to craft irresistible headlines:

- How To [Achieve Results] Without [Common Pain Point] - *Example: How To Lose 15 Pounds Without Going On Crazy Fad Diets*

- The Quickest Way To [Achieve Results] - *Example: The Quickest Way To Teach Your Child How To Read*

- [Achieve Results] In [Timeframe] - *Example: Learn To Speak Fluent Spanish In Just Four Weeks!*

- Revealed: The Secret To [Achieve Results] – *Example: Revealed: The Secret To Making Big Passive Income Through Your Blog*

- Get Rid of [Problem] Once and For All - *Example: Get Rid Of Your Bad Eating Habits Once and For All!*

- [Achieve Results] And [Desirable Circumstance] - *Example: Fine-Tune These Leadership Skills and Be the Boss*

- [Do Something] Like [World-Class Example] - *Example: Work Out Like An Olympian*

- Have A [Results] You Can Be Proud Of - *Example: Have A Body You Can Be Proud Of*

You can mix and match different elements of these headline formulas to create the perfect headline for your sales page.

Just be sure that your headline is specific, interesting, and speaks to the problem. Remember, your headline is what will convince people to read the rest of the sales page. Spend the necessary time crafting a headline worthy of the product or service that you're selling.

Step #3: Address Core Problems and Frustrations

Now it's time to start writing the actual copy of your sales page. The first thing to do is to highlight the pain points that your potential customers are already feeling. Your goal is to make them feel their pain points more acutely. To speak to the frustrations and challenges they're experiencing.
You want them to know that you understand where they're coming from. That you can relate to their struggles.

Be as specific as possible when highlighting the pain points. Use language that they use to describe the problems. You're trying to get the reader to think about how difficult and frustrating things currently are for them. You want them to ponder how things might be different in their lives.

Think of it like you're creating a "Before/After" scenario. In the "Before" scenario, you're painting a picture of what their life is currently like.

For example, you might say things like:

- Sick of spending money on Facebook ads and not getting any return?
- Building an online business is really difficult.
- Are you struggling to get consistent leads for your business?
- Few things are more difficult than losing belly fat.
- Saving for retirement shouldn't be this hard.
- Networking can be exhausting if you're an introvert.

When writing this section, go into as much detail as possible. Use vivid language and try to paint a picture. You want the reader to actively *feel* their pain points as you describe them. You want them to feel like you're talking directly to them.

Don't skimp on this section. Make it as long as needed to adequately convey the pain points and frustrations that your potential customers are feeling.

Step #4: Introduce Your Solution

Once you've sufficiently agitated the pain points, it's time to introduce the solution you offer. This is when you tell potential customers about the product or service you offer. You've spent a lot of time talking about their specific pain points and struggles. Now you offer your product or service as the perfect remedy to their problems.
When talking about your solution, start by talking about the benefits. Talk about how your product or service will absolutely change the lives of your potential customers. How it will solve their most painful problems and alleviate their deepest frustrations. Paint a picture of the good life that people will experience if they use your product or service.

The truth is that people are primarily interested in the *outcome* rather than your exact product or service. They care the most about how their life will change, not the exact methods you will use to change it.

Yes, you'll talk about those things, but not right away. You start by talking about the *benefits* of your product or service, not the features.

For example:

- Finally, you can know exactly how much ROI you'll get from Facebook ads.
- You can stop obsessively counting calories and start eating what you enjoy.
- Stop struggling to attract new customers and start bringing them in automatically.
- Easily scale your business to six-figures without killing yourself.
- Land your dream job at your dream company.
- You can stop being unproductive and start crushing your goals.

Your primary goal is to show potential customers just how fantastic their life will be if they adopt your solution. You want them to be convinced that your product or service is exactly what they need to solve their problems.

Once you've spent a significant amount of time talking about the benefits of your solution, then you can go into specific details about the features.

For example, maybe you offer done-for-you content creation. Or maybe part of your solution is three consulting calls. Or maybe you provide customers with detailed analysis of their financial situation.

Spell out in detail exactly how your solution works. You want potential customers to understand exactly what they're getting when they decide to work with you.

If you're selling a product, include plenty of photos (and possibly videos) of it. If it's a digital product, include screenshots. If you offer bonuses, like access to an exclusive online group, be crystal clear about those as well.

When talking about the features of your product or service, your goal is to help the reader become an informed buyer. Remember, they can't physically touch or see the product or service on your sales page. The more information you can include about it, the more potential buyers will trust you.

Step #5:
Make Your Offer

By this point, you've highlighted the pain points and talked about the benefits and features of your solution. Now it's time to actually make your offer. It's time to directly invite the reader to purchase from you or secure your services.

This will come in the form of a direct call-to-action.

The potential customer understands what you have to offer and why it's the perfect solution to their problems. Now you need to call them to take action on what they know.

Many times, it's good to put the CTA in the first person. This emphasizes to the potential customer that *they're the ones* taking action. It puts them in an action mindset and galvanizes them.

Some examples of strong calls-to-action include:

- I'm Ready To Start Crushing Facebook Ads!
- I'm In!

- Let's Do This
- Give Me Immediate Access
- I'm Ready To Start Saving
- Sign Me Up For The Networking Masterclass

Notice that all of these calls-to-action use strong, action-oriented words. You don't want your CTA to be weak, boring, or uninspired. You want the reader of your sales page to feel like they're doing something *big and important* when they click on your CTA.

Don't beat around the bush with your CTA. Make it direct and to the point. Make it clear that you want the potential customer to actually *do* something. Remember, you're *selling something*. If the potential customer doesn't take action and purchase, then your sales page fails.

Bottom line: You can't be afraid of asking people to buy.

Ask boldly and directly.

Step #6: Introduce Yourself

If people are going to purchase from you, they need to know who you are. They need to know why they should trust you. You have to give them a good reason to part with their hard earned money.

That's why you should create a section in which you introduce yourself. In this section, you're going to tell potential customers about who you are, why you're uniquely qualified to solve their problems, and why they should trust you.

In this section, consider including things like:

- A high-resolution photo of yourself
- Your experience
- Successes you've had
- High-profile clients you've worked with
- Degrees or certifications you hold
- Media appearances

For example, if you're an entrepreneur who's built multiple six-figure businesses, talk about that. If you've consulted for celebrities or well-known businesses, make that clear as well. If you've been featured on Forbes or SUCCESS or MSNBC, spell that out.

Don't be modest when writing this section.

You want to make it clear that you're an expert in your field and that you have the necessary experience to solve the problems people are facing.

Think of this section as an abbreviated resume. Your goal is to show off your knowledge and experience so that people trust you.

Step #7: Use Testimonials

Testimonials are an incredibly powerful form of social proof. Think about when you shop on Amazon. What's one of the first things you do? You look at the reviews to see how customers feel about the product. The truth is that we trust the words of others.

On your sales page, use testimonials from satisfied customers. They are especially helpful in overcoming objections and doubts that prospects may have. They feel authentic and prove that you've actually helped people. Testimonials back up the claims you make in your sales page and prove that your product or service actually works.

If you don't have many testimonials, ask existing, happy customers if they'd be willing to provide them for you.

Here are some specific questions you can ask customers to get powerful testimonials:

- What were you struggling with before you used my product or service?

- What specific results did you see as a result of using my product or service?
- Why would you recommend my product or service to others?
- What specific features of my product or service did you like?

The best testimonials are very specific in the details. For example, a testimonial that says, “This is a great product!” is good. A testimonial that says, “This product improved our conversion rate by 11%!” is much better.

It’s hard to overstate the importance of testimonials. They play a significant role in convincing people to buy and can dramatically improve your conversion rate. Take the necessary time to collect and curate powerful testimonials from your customers. Then use those testimonials on your sales page.

Step #8: Filter Out the Wrong People

Believe it or not, your sales page shouldn't appeal to everyone. You're selling a specific product or service that is geared toward a very specific audience. You're not Apple, trying to sell a product that is designed for the masses. The simple truth is that not everyone should be your customer.

Ideally, your sales page should filter out those who aren't a good fit for your offer.
Why is this so important? Because if the wrong people sign up for your offer, they become dissatisfied customers. Dissatisfied customers often want refunds, which creates a big headache for you.

Also, you only want to work with those who you can effectively serve. If the wrong people sign up for your offer, you'll both become frustrated when you discover that you're not a good fit for each other.

So how do you filter out the wrong people? By telling readers *exactly who* your offer is right for.

What characterizes your ideal customer? Are you targeting small business owners that make over $100,000 year? Or executives who are struggling to keep up with the demands of their job? Or people who struggle to keep their eating habits under control? Or older couples on the verge of retirement?

On your sales page, make it crystal clear who will be a good fit for your offer. List the things that characterize them.

For example, you could say something like:

> *Who is this for?*
>
> *It's for small business owners who make over $100k in revenue but aren't able to consistently generate leads. It's for entrepreneurs who want to use the power of online marketing to scale their business. It's for those who are desperate to grow their businesses but don't really know how.*

Notice how each element of the above paragraph narrows the ideal audience. The first sentence specifies that the offer is for business owners making over $100k. The second sentence specifies that it's for those who want to use online marketing. And the third sentence makes it clear that the ideal customer is the business owner who is desperate to grow.

Be very specific when it comes to defining who your offer is for. The more specific you can be, the more you'll attract your perfect customer and turn away those who aren't a great fit.

Step #9: Answer Frequently Asked Questions

Your potential customers will undoubtedly have questions as they read your sales page. The more you can directly answer their questions, the more you'll overcome their objections and the more likely it is that they'll buy from you.

What sorts of questions will people have regarding your offer?

Here are some common ones you may encounter:

- Are there any prerequisites?
- Do you offer a payment plan?
- How long does it normally take to see results?
- Is any special equipment needed?
- How do people receive your product?
- How long do they have access to your product?
- What payment types do you accept?

Try to put yourself in the shoes of those reading your sales page. What do you want to know before you purchase a product or service like yours? What would hold you back from buying? What is most important for you to know?

One way to figure out what questions people may have is to ask your existing customers what questions they had before they purchased from you. Have them help you identify the common questions people have regarding your product or service.

It's really important to be as thorough as possible when creating your FAQ section. Unanswered questions keep people from buying. They are an obstacle to sales. Do your best to anticipate any questions people might have and then provide thorough, satisfactory answers to those questions.

Also, put your contact information on your sales page so that your prospects can follow up with you if they have further questions.

Step #10: Add Urgency

If at all possible, add a sense of urgency to your sales page. You want to create a Fear Of Missing Out (FOMO) in people. You want them to feel like if they don't take action right away, they'll miss out on a great opportunity.

Additionally, adding urgency to your sales page forces people to make a decision. They can't indefinitely put off purchasing. They need to decide whether they're in or out.

Adding urgency to your sales page can significantly increase the conversion rate.

So how do you add urgency to your page?

There are several ways you can do this:

1. Offer your product or service for a limited time. For example, let's say you're selling an online course. You could open enrollment for your course for a short time, like two weeks.

2. Only take on a limited number of clients. For example, if you're a success coach,

you could limit yourself to taking on a maximum of ten clients at a time. Once you reach that limit, you refuse to take on any more.

3. Offer bonuses that expire after a set time. For example, if you're releasing a book, you could offer free digital downloads to everyone who buys the book in the first two weeks.

4. Limit the number of products you sell. For example, if you make handmade products, you could limit the number you make.

When adding urgency, it's really important that you stick to your promises. If you say you're only taking on 10 new clients, don't keep taking on new clients after 10. People will stop believing you if they find out that you created *artificial urgency.*

So, do what you say you're going to do when it comes to adding urgency to your offer.

Step #11:
Reiterate the Benefits and Call-To-Action

The final step in creating a killer sales page is to reiterate the benefits and again call the reader to take action.

When reiterating the benefits, help people imagine how their lives will change for the better if they adopt your product or service. Help them contrast the way things currently are to the way things will be.

Force them to decide whether they want things to remain as they are or whether they're ready for a positive change.

For example, you could say things like:

- Are you ready to finally stop struggling to get leads and to start easily scaling your business?

- How would it change your life if you could easily manage all the information coming your way every day?

- It's time to finally take back control of your life and change your eating habits.

- If you're ready to finally start building your retirement nest egg, today is the day to take action.

- It's time to live the life you deserve. To stop struggling to lose weight and be your best, healthy self.

You want to reinforce just how effective your product or solution really is. You want people to feel like they'll be missing out if they *don't* purchase your product or service.

After you've reiterated the benefits, it's time to make a final call-to-action. You again want to tell the reader to take action. If they've read this far in your sales page, it probably means they're interested in what you have to offer. But they haven't yet responded to your call-to-action. This is your last chance to get them to buy from you.

Like with your previous call-to-action, be direct and to the point. Don't beat around the bush. Make it very clear and obvious what you want the reader to do. If you're using a button for your call-to-action, make the button big and obvious.

The Importance of Subheadings and Scannable Copy

Your sales page should be easy to read - so much so that a person could skim through it and get a good feel for your offer.

No one likes to look at solid blocks of text. They don't want to have to carefully read every single word in order to understand what you're offering.

So how do you make your sales page easily readable? By using plenty of subheadings, paragraph breaks, and bullet points.

A good rule of thumb is that *each* new section in your sales page should have its own subheading. When you address the core problems and frustrations, lead into that section with a subheading. When you make your offer, use a subheading. Use a subheading when you introduce yourself.

When writing your subheadings, follow the same rules as when writing your overall headline:

- Each subheading should be interesting and keep the reader moving down the page.

- Each one should draw the reader in and make them want to see what comes next.

- And subheadings should be clear enough that a person can get a sense of the entire sales page just from reading them.

Within each section, ensure that the copy itself is easy to skim. Use short paragraphs. Every few sentences, start a new paragraph. This allows a person to quickly move down the page and get a good feel for what you're saying. If they want to closely study individual sections, they can always come back and do that.

After you've written a complete draft of your sales page, quickly skim through it yourself. Is it easy on the eyes? Can most of the information be taken in at a brief glance? Are there any areas where you're forced to slow down in order to understand the content?

Do your best to make the entire sales page smooth and easy to read. The overall result will be happier readers, which in turn leads to higher conversion rates.

Putting It All Together

Now you know all the elements of a successful sales page. You know the "formula." All that's left is to put all these things together into one highly compelling sales page.

The killer sales page formula is as follows:

- Understand your audience
- Craft your headline
- Address the core problems and frustrations
- Introduce your solution
- Make your offer
- Introduce yourself
- Use testimonials
- Filter out the wrong people
- Answers FAQs
- Add urgency
- Reiterate the benefits and call-to-action
- Use subheadings and scannable copy

Each of these elements is essential to a great sales page. If you leave any of them out, your conversion rate will probably decrease, leading to lower overall sales numbers. However, when you bring all these elements together, the end result is a highly compelling, extremely interesting, revenue-generating sales page.

Now it's time for us to give *you* a call-to-action.

You know how to write a killer sales page that converts like crazy. You know the formula for success. All that's left is for you to get started.

So get out there and write that sales page!

EXCLUSIVE OFFER

You took action to take control of your income and future, and for that I want to give you an exclusive offer only available to those who purchase this book.

There is much work ahead, and I want to help you get there.

That is why I developed the Brand Awareness Accelerator Training, a step-by-step training course to help you get the attention of your target audience and position your business at the top of their minds.

Below is a coupon code for you to get 50% off this training.

BONUS: When you purchase the training using the code below, you will also receive a complimentary coaching call where I will help you set goals and milestones to ensure your success.

Register at: growth.getmindmagnet.com

Use Code: killersales

Made in United States
North Haven, CT
04 November 2026

21767741R00024